JOKES for KIDS

ANIMALS.
ROAD TRIPS.
RIDDLES.
KNOCK-KNOCK JOKES.

CHANTELLE GRACE

Broadstreet

BroadStreet Kids
Savage, Minnesota, USA

BroadStreet Kids is an imprint of
BroadStreet Publishing Group, LLC.
Broadstreetpublishing.com

JOKES FOR KIDS-BUNDLE TWO

9781424566549

Design and typesetting | garborgdesign.com
Compiled and edited by Michelle Winger | literallyprecise.com

Printed in China.

23   24   25   26   27   28   7   6   5   4   3   2   1

Author Bio

CHANTELLE GRACE is a witty wordsmith who loves music, art, and competitive games. She is fascinated by God's intricate design of the human body, and, as a nurse, she knows it's important to share the gift of laughter with those around her.

TABLE OF CONTENTS....

BEST ANIMAL JOKES EVER

BEST KNOCK-KNOCK JOKES EVER

BEST RIDDLES EVER

BEST ROAD TRIP JOKES EVER

BEST. ANIMAL JOKES. EVER.

JOKES for KIDS

CHANTELLE GRACE

HOUND HYSTERIA

What happened to the dog that swallowed a firefly?

It barked with de-light.

Why don't dogs make good dancers?

Because they have two left feet.

When is a dog not a dog?

When it is pure bred.

What dog keeps the best time?

A watch dog.

What do you call a great dog detective?

Sherlock Bones.

What do you call young dogs who play in the snow?

Slush puppies.

What type of markets do dogs avoid?

Flea markets.

When does a dog go "moo"?

When it is learning a new language.

How did the little Scottish dog feel when it saw a monster?

It was Terrier-fied.

Where do Eskimos train their dogs?

In the mush room.

What dog loves to take bubble baths?

A shampoodle.

Why do you get if you cross a chili pepper, a shovel, and a terrier?

A hot-diggity-dog.

What did the dog say when it sat on sandpaper?

"Ruff."

What do dogs eat at the movies?

Pupcorn.

What did the Dalmatian say after eating dinner?

"That hit the spot."

What is a dog's favorite dessert?

Pupcakes.

What do you do if your dog chews a dictionary?

Take the words out of its mouth.

What kind of sports cars do dogs drive?

Furarris.

How do you say goodbye to a curly-haired dog?

"Poodle-oo."

Why did the poor dog chase its own tail?

It was trying to make ends meet.

How are dogs like phones?

They have collar IDs.

CAT COMEDY

What do cats eat for breakfast?

Mice Crispies.

What does a twenty-pound mouse say to a cat?

"Here kitty, kitty, kitty."

What is a cat's favorite color?

Purrple.

What animals are the best pets?

Cats, because they are purrfect.

What are caterpillars afraid of?

Doggerpillars.

What kind of cats like to go bowling?

Alley cats.

What do you call a pile of kittens?

A meowntain.

What is a cat's favorite song?

Three Blind Mice.

What is it called when a cat wins a dog show?

A cat-has-trophy.

Why are cats so good at video games?

Because they have nine lives.

What's a cat's favorite dessert?

Chocolate mouse.

What do you call a cat wearing shoes?

Puss in boots.

Why do cats always get their way?

They make a purrsuasive case.

What do you call a cat that's in trouble with the police?

A purrpetrator.

ARCTIC AMUSEMENT

Who is the penguin's favorite Aunt?

   Aunt Arctica.

What's white, furry, and shaped like a tooth?

   A molar bear.

What's a penguin's favorite salad?

Iceberg lettuce.

Why did the penguin cross the road?

To go with the floe.

Where do penguins go to the movies?

At the dive-in.

How does a penguin make pancakes?

With its flippers.

Where do polar bears vote?

The North Poll.

Where do penguins go to dance?

The snow ball.

What do penguins have for lunch?

Icebergers.

Why don't you see penguins in the United Kingdom?

Because they're afraid of Wales.

How does a penguin build its house?

Igloos it together.

What do you get when you cross a walrus with a bee?

A wallaby.

How do penguins drink?

Out of beakers.

What do penguins wear on their heads?

Ice caps.

What do you get when you cross a penguin and an alligator?

I don't know, but don't try to fix its bow tie.

SEA LIFE SHENANIGANS

What does a shark like to eat with peanut butter?

Jellyfish.

What do you get when you cross fish and an elephant?

Swimming trunks.

How many tickles does it take to make an octopus laugh?

Ten-tickles.

What is a shark's favorite sci-fi show?

Shark Trek.

Why is a fish easy to weigh?

Because it has its own scales.

What do you call a solitary shark?

A lone shark.

What fish only swims at night?

A starfish.

Why are there some fish at the bottom of the ocean?

Because they dropped out of school.

Why don't sharks like fast food?

Because they can't catch it.

What do you call a fish without an eye?

A fsh.

What did the shark say to the whale?

"What are you blubbering about?"

Where do fish sleep?

On a seabed.

What is the strongest creature
in the sea?

A mussel.

Where do fish go when their things
go missing?

The Lost-and-Flounder Department.

How do oysters call their friends?

On shell phones.

What's the difference between a guitar and a fish?

You can't tuna fish.

Why do fish live in saltwater?

Because pepper makes them sneeze.

What do fish do at football games?

They wave.

What does a fish do in a crisis?

Sea-kelp.

Okay that's enough fish puns.

It's time to scale back.

JUNGLE JEST

Why do gorillas have big nostrils?

Because they have big fingers.

How does a lion greet the other animals in the field?

"Pleased to eat you."

Why did the monkey like the banana?

Because it had appeal.

Why don't you have to tell an elephant a secret more than once?

Because elephants never forget.

Why didn't the boy believe the tiger?

He thought it was a lion.

What did the banana say to the monkey?

Nothing. Bananas can't talk.

Why are elephants so wrinkled?

They take too long to iron.

What kind of jungle cat is no fun to play games with?

A cheetah.

What do monkeys do for laughs?

They tell jokes about people.

How do you get down off an elephant?

You don't, you get down off a duck.

When is a well-dressed lion like a weed?

When he's a dandelion.

What sport don't you want to play with an elephant?

Squash.

Where do chimps get their information?

From the ape vine.

How do you raise a baby elephant?

With a forklift.

How do monkeys get down the stairs?

They slide down the bananaster.

Why are elephants so poor?

Because they work for peanuts.

What animal gets in trouble at school?

The cheetah.

What's black and white and blue?

A sad zebra.

Why can't a leopard hide?

Because he's always spotted.

Why did the elephant stay in the airport?

It was waiting for its trunk.

FARM FUNNIES

What do you get if you cross a chicken with a cow?

Roost beef.

What do you get from a pampered cow?

Spoiled milk.

What type of horses only go out at night?

Nightmares.

What do you get when a chicken lays an egg on top of a barn?

An eggroll.

What did the pony say when it had a sore throat?

"I'm a little hoarse."

Why can't you shock cows?

They've herd it all.

Why didn't the chicken cross the road?

Because there was a KFC on the other side.

What do you get when you cross a sheep and a honeybee?

Baahumbug.

What do you call a dancing sheep?

A baallerina.

What do you call a sheep that is always quiet?

A shhhheep.

Why did the pig become an actor?

Because he was a ham.

Why did the chicken cross the road?

To show everyone he wasn't chicken.

What kind of pigs know karate?

Pork chops.

What kind of ties do pigs wear?

Pigsties.

How do Hispanic sheep say
Merry Christmas?

"Fleece Navidad."

How many sheep does it take to knit
a sweater?

Don't be silly; sheep can't knit.

What do you call cattle with a sense of humor?

Laughing stock.

What animal sounds like a sheep but isn't?

A baaboon.

Why was the sheep pulled over on the freeway?

Because she did a ewe turn.

What do you get if you cross an angry sheep and a grumpy cow?

An animal that's in a baad moood.

How do chickens bake a cake?

From scratch.

What do you call a cow with two legs?

Lean beef.

What do you give a sick pig?

Oinkment.

What do you call a cow with no legs?

Ground beef.

Why did the piece of gum cross
the road?

It was stuck to the chicken's foot.

What do you get if you cross a cocker
spaniel, a poodle, and a rooster?

"Cockerpoodledoo."

What do you call a sleeping cow?

A bulldozer.

If fruit comes from a fruit tree, where does chicken come from?

A poultree.

Why was the cow afraid?

He was a cow-herd.

What do you call a cow that just had a baby?

Decalfinated.

Where do milkshakes come from?

Nervous cows.

What do you call a cow spying on another cow?

A steak out.

What did the teacher say when the horse walked into the class?

"Why the long face?"

What did the horse say when it fell?

"I've fallen and I can't giddyup."

What goes, "Oooooooo."

A cow with no lips.

What did the mama cow say to the baby cow?

"It's pasture bedtime."

How do horses stay in such great shape?

They keep a stable diet.

What day do chickens fear the most?

Fryday.

Why did Mozart get rid of his chickens?

They kept saying, "Bach, Bach!"

FOREST FOOLERY

How do bears keep their den cool in summer?

They use bear conditioning.

Why was the rabbit so upset?

It was having a bad hare day.

What do you call a bear with no teeth?

A gummy bear.

What has 12 legs, six eyes, three tails, and can't see?

Three blind mice.

How do you know that carrots are good for your eyesight?

Rabbits never wear glasses.

What do you call a bear with no ear?

B.

What is an owl's favorite subject?

Owlgebra.

Why are teddy bears never hungry?

They are always stuffed.

What's gray, squeaky and lives in caves?

Stalagmice.

What do you call an owl with a deep voice?

A growl.

How do you save a deer during hunting season?

You hang on for deer life.

What do you get if you cross a bear with a pig?

A teddy boar.

Why did the owl say, "Tweet, tweet"?

Because she didn't give a hoot.

What kind of book does a rabbit like to read?

One with a hoppy ending.

What is a baby owl after it is six days old?

Seven days old.

Why do male deer need braces?

Because they have buck teeth.

How do rabbits stay in shape?

They do a lot of hareobics.

How do you catch a squirrel?

Climb up a tree and act like a nut.

How can you tell which are the oldest rabbits?

Just look for the gray hares.

Who did Bambi invite to his birthday party?

His nearest and deerest friends.

How do mice feel when they are sick?

Mouserable.

What do you call a wet baby owl?

A moist owlette.

What do you call a bear caught in the rain?

A drizzly bear.

Why did the owl invite its friends over?

It didn't want to be owl by itself.

Where do mice park their boats?

At the hickory dickory dock.

What did the judge say when the skunk came into his courtroom?

"Odor in the court."

POND PLAY

What happens when a frog parks in a no-parking space?

It gets toad away.

What do you call a crate of ducks?

A box of quackers.

What is a frog's favorite exercise?

Jumping jacks.

Who stole the soap?

The robber ducky.

Why are frogs so happy?

They eat whatever bugs them.

What do you get when you cross a frog and a bunny?

A ribbit.

What animal has more lives than a cat?

Frogs. They croak every night.

What did the duck say when buying lipstick?

"Put it on my bill."

What did one frog say to the other?

"Time is fun when you're having flies."

What time does a duck wake up?

At the quack of dawn.

What is a frog's favorite music?

Hip hop.

What do you get if you cross a frog and a dog?

A croaker spaniel.

What happens when a duck flies upside down?

It quacks up.

What is a frog's favorite hot drink?

Hot croak-o.

What goes dot-dot-croak, dot-dash-croak?

A morse toad.

Which animal grows down?

A duck.

What do ducks watch on TV?

Duckumentaries.

What do you call a frog with no hind legs?

Unhoppy.

Where do frogs leave their hats and coats?

In the croakroom.

What do you call a duck who leads an orchestra?

A conducktor.

What is a frog's favorite cold drink?

Croak-a-cola.

What does a duck like to eat with soup?

Quackers.

What do frogs wear on their feet?

Open toad shoes.

What did the duck wear to his wedding?

A duxedo.

What do you get when you cross a frog and a popsicle?

A hopsicle.

What do you get if you cross fireworks with a duck?

A fire quacker.

CREEPY CAPERS

What snakes are found on cars?

Windshield vipers.

Why did the snake cross the road?

To get to the other ssside.

What do you get when you cross
a snake and a pastry?

A pie-thon.

Why are snakes hard to fool?

You can't pull their leg.

What do you call a snake with a great
personality?

A snake charmer.

What do you call an alligator with a spy glass?

An investigator.

What is a snake's favorite school subject?

Hissstory.

What do you call a thieving alligator?

A crook-o-dile.

How do bees get to school?

By school buzz.

Two flies are on the porch. Which one is an actor?

The one on the screen.

What is the biggest ant in the world?

An elephant.

Why didn't the butterfly go to the dance?

Because it was a moth ball.

When did the fly fly?

When the spider spied her.

What do you call two ants that run away to get married?

Antelopes.

How do fleas travel from place to place?

They itchhike.

What is an insect's favorite sport?

Cricket.

Why did the kid throw the butter out the window?

To see the butterfly.

What kind of fly has a frog in its throat?

A hoarse fly.

Why was the bee's hair sticky?

Because it used a honeycomb.

SOARING SILLIES

What's yellow, weighs 1,000 pounds, and sings?

Two 500-pound canaries.

Where does a peacock go when it loses its tail?

A retail store.

Why does a flamingo stand on one leg?

Because if it lifted that leg off the ground, it would fall down.

What kind of bird can carry the most weight?

The crane.

Did you hear the story about the peacock?

It's a beautiful tale.

What bird is with you at every meal?

A swallow.

What do you give a sick bird?

Tweetment.

Why do birds fly south for the winter?

Because it's too far to walk.

Why do hummingbirds hum?

Because they forgot the words.

What bird is always sad?

The blue jay.

What's noisier than a whooping crane?

A trumpeting swan.

What do you call a bird in the winter?

Brrrd.

What do you get if you cross a canary and a 50-foot-long snake?

A sing-a-long.

What do you get when you cross a parrot and a shark?

A bird that talks your ear off.

What do you get when you cross a snowman with a vampire bat?

Frostbite.

Why did the canary sit on the ladder to sing?

It wanted to reach the high notes.

Why did the birdie go to the candy store?

It wanted a tweet.

Why do seagulls fly over the sea?

Because if they flew over the bay, they would be bagels.

HINKETY PINKETY

Wouldn't it be funny if
we called a bumblebee a *fuzzy buzzy?*
Or a hippo a *floatie bloaty?*
A parrot could be a *wordy birdy,*
and a cat a *furry purry.*
If a dog were a *fluffy ruffy,*
a beluga could be a *pale whale,*
and a wasp a *wingy stingy.*

Your pet caretaker, or *critter sitter,*
would make for a happier dog—
a *merrier terrier* or a *jolly collie.*
A miniature sausage dog,
we'll call it a *teeny weenie,*

takes a bath and becomes a *soggy doggy*,
then lets out a bark or other *hound sound*.
That awakens the clever cat, or *witty kitty*,
who licks her paw warmer, her *kitten mitten*,
and begins searching for the rodent home,
aka *mouse house*,
and hopes for the chubbiest member,
the *fat rat*, to come out.
Sometimes the other rodent,
the *mouse spouse*, peeks its head out.
But most of the time,
it's the bushy-tailed spin, or *squirrel twirl*,
outside that catches the cat's eye.

When the slippery fowl, *slick chick*,
is up to her tricks,
you'll see another bird frown.
That's an *owl scowl*.
The runaway honker is a real *loose goose*.
It speeds past a lazy black bird, the *slow crow*,
and rushes by the casual parrot, or *walkie talkie*.
A royal raptor, *regal eagle*, takes to the skies
while pink birds chatter using *flamingo lingo*,
and the math-loving pelican, or *nerdy birdy*,
keeps an eye out for a sushi plate—a *fish dish*.
A quick dip in the water requires a bird dryer,
like an *owl towel*.

The sea lion should sign a contract, a *seal deal*,
with the hammerhead tattletale, the *narc shark*.
The blue-green moray, or *teal eel*,
could borrow the sea cow's mirror,
the *manatee vanity*,
to check his patient's arctic tooth—
polar molar.

A wheeled reptile might prefer to be labeled
a *skater gator*,
and it may have to dodge a tortoise
obstacle, or *turtle hurdle*, along the way.
Hopefully if it runs into a snowstorm,
a *lizard blizzard*,
it would take time to rest—*snake break*.
A magical reptile, or *wizard lizard*,
could turn a tool, a *snake rake*, into a shovel,
and hand it to an energetic hisser,
or *hyper viper*.

If you come across a cow stealer,
you might call him a *beef thief*.
At the same farm, you may encounter
a fake horse, or *phony pony*.
Of course, there's the hog with the
hairpiece, the *pig wig*,

and that super frugal lamb—*cheap sheep*—
with an unpleasant odor or *ewe pew*.
They all need the help of a lawful bird,
a *legal eagle*,
who sometimes wears a pest suit, or
mosquito tuxedo.

In the forest, a hare comedian,
the *funny bunny*,
sticks to its routine, or *rabbit habit*.
The mink offspring, *otter daughter*,
prefers to use the art stand,
the *weasel easel*,
to capture a marvelous marsupial—
the *awesome possum*.
Meanwhile, in the smelly animal bed,
or *skunk bunk*,
lies the mohawked stinker, the *punk skunk*,
who has stolen the canine's footwarmers,
or *fox socks*.

The spicy feline, *peppered leopard*,
fixes a cat sandwich, or *cheetah pita*,
and pours a drink into a long-necked
pitcher—a *giraffe carafe*.
That attracts the chubby chimp,
the *chunky monkey*,

who races over in a ring-tailed sportscar,
or *lemur beamer,*
leaving the cream-colored ape,
vanilla gorilla, behind.
On the way, it passes a sad wildebeest,
a *blue gnu,*
and an emotional feline, a *cryin' lion.*
What a wild mess—a real *jungle bungle!*

TITLE TRICKS

Hot Dog

by Frank Furter

Cry Wolf

by Al Armist

Beekeeping

by A. P. Arry

I Like Fish

by Ann Chovie

Turtle Racing

by Eubie Quick

Off to Market

by Tobias A. Pigg

Mosquito Bites

by Ivan Itch

Desert Crossing

by I. Rhoda Camel

Those Funny Dogs

by Joe Kur

Crocodile Dundee

by Ali Gator

Let's Do That Now

by Igor Beaver

Animal Illnesses

by Ann Thrax

Smashing Lobster

by Buster Crabbe

The Unknown Rodent

by A. Nonny Mouse

Snakes of the World

by Anna Conda

A Whole Lot of Cats

by Kitt N. Caboodle

WILDLIFE
WISECRACKS

If you're looking for great animal puns,

paws what you're doing and read these.

Raining cats and dogs is ok, as long as it doesn't...

reindeer.

The dad buffalo was sad when his male child left for college.

His parting words were,

"Bison."

Someone told me to get along little doggy,

so I bought a dachshund.

It was okay that the dolphin made a mistake.

He said he didn't do it on...

porpoise.

At first I wondered why cows had hooves instead of feet,

but then I realized it's because they...

lactose.

Crabs never give to charity because they are...

shellfish.

The veterinarian was sad when the monkey cut off its tail.

She said,

"It won't be long now."

An elephant stopped in the middle of telling a story...

never mind; it's irrelephant.

After the fish proposed an idea, he concluded with,

"Let minnow what you think."

The embarrassed bird of prey fell off a tree branch in front of a bunch of other birds.

It was really hawkward.

I find puns about pigs a little...

boaring.

The bird got arrested for stealing from the doctor.

What it was doing was...

ill-eagle.

It was strange to see the panda in a tank top.

But he does have the right to...

bear arms.

Someone said I sounded like an owl.

"Who?"

I asked everyone what happened to the lost cattle.

Nobody's herd.

The biggest goal of the detective duck was to...

quack the case.

The pig lied about taking a bath.

The farmer said, "Hogwash."

So it did.

Simba was walking too slowly so I told him to...

Mufasa.

Why isn't a koala a bear if he has all the necessary...

koalifications?

When you're down in the sea and an eel bites your knee...

that's a moray.

The farmer called the cow with no milk an...

udder failure.

It was raining cats and dogs when I walked outside.

I stepped in a poodle.

I saw a cow on stilts the other day.

The steaks have been raised.

If there's a problem at the beaver dam,

get otter here.

Whenever we go sightseeing in the ocean, I find myself saying,

"Whale, hello there."

Did you hear about the bear anarchy?

It was a pandamonium.

If a prize is won for coming in last, tortoises are...

turtley the best.

Sea lions love surfing?

That's the sealiest thing I've ever heard.

I tried to get the dog to bark,
but it was a...

hush puppy.

Boring bees are annoying.

They drone on and on.

All those people out there wanting to
swim with the sea cows?

Oh, the humanatee.

Dogs at a construction site are best at...

roofing.

Board meetings with horses are useless.

They always vote neigh.

That owl does magic tricks?

It must be Hoodini.

I was shocked when a chicken ordered a drink at Starbucks.

It must have been an...

eggspresso.

I don't remember the specifics,
but Pavlov's theory...

rings a bell.

Sometimes the best way to
communicate with fish is to...

drop them a line.

A man was hospitalized with six plastic
horses in his stomach.

The doctor said his condition was...

stable.

When you go on a safari,
take a good book.

Then you can read...

between the lions.

Australian bears hang out in trees
together.

Their love language is...

koalaty time.

I thought I would like deer hunting,
but I realized in the end I wasn't really...

fawned of it.

I caught a blue marlin.

I should probably listen to this fish.

It has a point.

I don't see what the big deal is about the black bird.

But people keep...

raven.

The lion exhibit at the zoo is quite popular.

I guess it's the...

mane attraction.

I don't know why people don't laugh at the large deer.

I find him pretty...

amoosing.

The prairie dog is really no big deal.

He's a...

meerkat.

The orca is an amazing actor.

It does a...

killer whale impersonation.

BEST.
Knock-knock
JOKES.
EVER

JOKES for KIDS

CHANTELLE GRACE

ANIMAL ANTICS

Knock, knock.

Who's there?

Hoo.

Hoo who?

You talk like an owl.

Knock, knock.

Who's there?

Goat.

Goat who?

Goat on a limb and open the door.

Knock, knock.

Who's there?

Lion.

Lion who?

Lion on your doorstep. Open up.

Knock, knock.

Who's there?

Dragon.

Dragon who?

Dragon your feet again?

Knock, knock.

Who's there?

Duck.

Duck who?

Just duck. They're throwing things at us.

Knock, knock.

Who's there?

Roach.

Roach who?

Roach you an email last week and haven't heard back.

Knock, knock.

Who's there?

Kanga.

Kanga who?

No, it's kangaroo.

Knock, knock.

Who's there?

Toucan.

Toucan who

Toucan play that game.

Knock, knock.

Who's there?

Alpaca.

Alpaca who?

Alpaca the suitcase; you load the car.

Knock, knock.

Who's there?

Wood ant.

Wood ant who?

Wood ant harm a fly; don't worry.

Knock, knock.

Who's there?

Owl.

Owl who?

Owl good things come to those who wait.

Knock, knock.

Who's there?

Fleas.

Fleas who?

Fleas a jolly good fellow.

Knock, knock.

Who's there?

Honeybee.

Honeybee who?

Honeybee a doll and open the door.

Knock, knock.

Who's there?

Rhino.

Rhino who?

Rhino every knock-knock joke there is.

Knock, knock.

Who's there?

Rabbit.

Rabbit who?

Rabbit up carefully; it's fragile.

Knock, knock.

Who's there?

Herd.

Herd who?

Herd you were home, so can you come out?

Knock, knock.

Who's there?

Bee.

Bee who?

Bee at my house at hive-o-clock.

Knock, knock.

Who's there?

Gorilla.

Gorilla who?

Gorilla me a hamburger, please.

Knock, knock.

Who's there?

Whale.

Whale who?

Whale, whale, whale, what do we have here?

Knock, knock.

Who's there?

Chimp.

Chimp who?

Chimp off the old block.

Knock, knock.

Who's there?

Herring.

Herring who?

Herring some awful knock-knock jokes.

Knock, knock.

Who's there?

Sore ewe.

Sore ewe who?

Sore ewe going to open the door or not?

Knock, knock.

Who's there?

Iguana.

Iguana who?

Iguana hold your hand.

Knock, knock.

Who's there?

Geese.

Geese who?

Geese what I'm going to do if you don't open the door?

Knock, knock.

Who's there?

Alligator.

Alligator who?

Alligator for her birthday was a card.

Knock, knock.

Who's there?

Bat.

Bat who?

Bat you'll never guess.

Knock, knock.

Who's there?

Howl.

Howl who?

Howl you know unless you open the door?

Why did the chicken cross the road?

To get to your house.

Knock, knock.

Who's there?

The chicken.

Knock, knock.

Who's there?

Cows go.

Cows go who?

No, cows go moo.

Knock, knock.

Who's there?

Bison.

Bison who?

Bison girl scout cookies, please.

Knock, knock.

Who's there.

Fangs.

Fangs who?

Fangs for letting me in.

Knock, knock.

Who's there?

Ruff.

Ruff who?

Ruff day. Let me in.

Knock, knock.

Who's there?

Owl.

Owl who?

Owl aboard.

Knock, knock.

Who's there?

Chimp.

Chimp who?

I think it's pronounced "shampoo."

Knock, knock.

Who's there?

Interrupting cow.

Interrupting cow wh...

Moo.

Knock, knock.

Who's there?

Laughing tentacles.

Laughing tentacles who?

You would laugh too if you had ten tickles.

Knock, knock.

Who's there?

Viper.

Viper who?

Viper nose; it's running.

NAME GAME

Knock, knock.

Who's there?

Luke.

Luke who?

Luke through the peephole and find out.

Knock, knock.

Who's there?

Duncan.

Duncan who?

*Duncan my cookies in milk.
Can you open the door?*

Knock, knock.

Who's there?

Goliath.

Goliath who?

Goliath down. You looketh tired.

Knock, knock.

Who's there?

Oswald.

Oswald who?

Oswald my bubblegum.

Knock, knock.

Who's there?

Teddy.

Teddy who?

Teddy is the beginning of the rest of your life.

Knock, knock.

Who's there?

Odysseus.

Odysseus who?

Odysseus the last straw.

Knock, knock.

Who's there?

Wendy.

Wendy who?

Wendy wind blows, it messes up my hair.

Knock, knock.

Who's there?

Ronde.

Ronde who?

Ronde vous here?

Knock, knock.

Who's there?

Barbara.

Barbara who?

Barbara black sheep, have you any wool?

Knock, knock.

Who's there?

Theresa.

Theresa who?

Theresa joke for everyone.

Knock, knock.

Who's there?

Rita.

Rita who?

Rita book of knock-knock jokes.

Knock, knock.

Who's there?

Alex.

Alex who?

Alex the questions around here.

Knock, knock.

Who's there?

Abbey.

Abbey who?

Abbey stung me on the arm.

Knock, knock.

Who's there?

Mikey.

Mikey who?

Mikey doesn't fit in the lock.

Knock, knock.

Who's there?

Rhoda.

Rhoda who?

*Rhoda long way to get here;
now open up.*

Knock, knock.

Who's there?

Avery.

Avery who?

*Avery time I come to your house,
we go through this.*

Knock, knock.

Who's there?

Mary.

Mary who?

Mary me?

Knock, knock.

Who's there?

Imena.

Imena who?

Imena pickle; open the door.

Knock, knock.

Who's there?

Noah.

Noah who?

Noah good place to eat?

Knock, knock.

Who's there?

Candice.

Candice who?

Candice door open or not?

Knock, knock.

Who's there?

Isma.

Isma who?

Isma lunch ready yet?

Knock, knock.

Who's there?

Alexia.

Alexia who?

Alexia again to open this door.

Knock, knock.

Who's there?

Toby.

Toby who?

Toby or not Toby, that is the question.

Knock, knock.

Who's there?

Abby.

Abby who?

Abby birthday to you.

Knock, knock.

Who's there?

Euripides.

Euripides who?

Euripides jeans; you pay for them.

Knock, knock.

Who's there?

Adolph.

Adolph who?

Adolph ball hit me in the mouth.

Knock, knock.

Who's there?

Aida.

Aida who?

Aida lot of sweets, and now I've got a tummy ache.

Knock, knock.

Who's there?

Horton hears a.

Horton hears a who?

I didn't know you liked Dr. Seuss.

Knock, knock.

Who's there?

Linda.

Linda who?

Linda hand, will you? Mine's tired from knocking.

Knock, knock.

Who's there?

Al.

Al who?

Al give you a hug if you open this door.

Knock, knock.

Who's there?

Aldo.

Aldo who?

Aldo anywhere with you.

Knock, knock.

Who's there?

Aladdin.

Aladdin who?

Aladdin the street wants a word with you.

Knock, knock.

Who's there?

Alec.

Alec who?

Alectricity. Isn't that a shock?

Knock, knock.

Who's there?

Anna.

Anna who?

Anna going to tell you.

Knock, knock.

Who's there?

Justin.

Justin who?

Justin time for dinner.

Knock, knock.

Who's there?

Doris.

Doris who?

Doris locked; that's why I knocked.

Knock, knock.

Who's there?

Aaron.

Aaron who?

Aaron you going to open the door?

Knock, knock.

Who's there?

Anita.

Anita who?

Anita borrow a key.

Knock, knock.

Who's there?

Alice.

Alice who?

Alice fair in love and war.

Knock, knock.

Who's there?

Nobel.

Nobel who?

Nobel. That's why I knocked.

Knock, knock.

Who's there?

Annie.

Annie who?

*Annie thing you can do,
I can do better.*

Knock, knock.

Who's there?

Theodore.

Theodore who?

Theodore is stuck, and it won't open.

Knock, knock.

Who's there?

Cher.

Cher who?

Cher would be nice if you opened the door.

Knock, knock

Who's there?

Amos.

Amos who?

Amos quito just bit me; hurry up.

Knock, knock.

Who's there?

Claire.

Claire who?

Claire a path; I'm coming through.

Knock, knock.

Who's there?

Norma Lee.

Norma Lee who?

Norma Lee I don't knock, but I am today.

Knock, knock.

Who's there?

Watson.

Watson who?

Watson TV? I'm coming in.

Knock, knock.

Who's there?

Iva.

Iva who?

*Iva sore hand from knocking.
Let me in.*

Knock, knock.

Who's there?

Sadie.

Sadie who?

Sadie magic word, and I'll come in.

Knock, knock.

Who's there?

Woo.

Woo who?

Oh, I'm so glad you're excited to see me.

Knock, knock.

Who's there?

Amanda.

Amanda who?

Amanda fix the lock on your door.

FOOD FRENZY

Knock, knock.

Who's there?

Cracker.

Cracker who?

*Cracker 'nother bad joke,
and I'm leaving.*

Knock, knock.

Who's there?

Butter.

Butter who?

Butter if you don't know.

Knock, knock?

Who's there?

Turnip.

Turnip who?

Turnip the volume; it's my favorite song.

Knock, knock.

Who's there?

Honeydew.

Honeydew who?

Honeydew you want to dance?

Knock, knock.

Who's there?

Lettuce.

Lettuce who?

Lettuce in, and you'll find out.

Knock, knock.

Who's there?

Ice cream.

Ice cream who?

Ice cream if you don't let me in.

Knock, knock.

Who's there?

Pecan.

Pecan who?

Pecan someone your own size.

Knock, knock.

Who's there?

Figs.

Figs who?

Figs the doorbell; it's broken.

Knock, knock.

Who's there?

Cereal.

Cereal who?

Cereal pleasure to meet you.

Knock, knock.

Who's there?

Pudding.

Pudding who?

Pudding this package right here for you.

Knock, knock.

Who's there?

Ketchup.

Ketchup who?

Ketchup to me, and I will tell you.

Knock, knock.

Who's there?

Orange.

Orange who?

Orange you going to answer the door?

Knock, knock.

Who's there?

Beets.

Beets who?

Beets me.

Knock, knock.

Who's there?

Muffin.

Muffin who?

Muffin the matter with me; how about you?

Knock, knock.

Who's there?

Olive.

Olive who?

Olive you.

Knock, knock.

Who's there?

Omelet.

Omelet who?

Omelet smarter than I look.

Knock, knock.

Who's there?

Doughnut.

Doughnut who?

Doughnut disturb me.

Knock, knock.

Who's there?

Carrot.

Carrot who?

Carrot all who this is?

Knock, knock.

Who's there?

Celery.

Celery who?

Celery isn't high enough. I quit.

Knock, knock.

Who's there?

Sultan.

Sultan who?

Sultan pepper.

Knock, knock.

Who's there?

Two fours.

Two fours who?

Two fours the door open would be bad.

Knock, knock.

Who's there?

Candy.

Candy who?

Candy cow jump over de moon?

Knock, knock.

Who's there?

Pasta.

Pasta who?

Pasta key, so I can open the door.

Knock, knock.

Who's there?

Thermos.

Thermos who?

Thermos be a better way to get a hold of you.

Knock, knock.

Who's there?

Cash.

Cash who?

No thanks, but I'd like some peanuts.

Knock, knock.

Who's there?

Broccoli.

Broccoli who?

Broccoli doesn't have a last name, silly.

Knock, knock.

Who's there?

Eggs.

Eggs who?

Eggscited to meet you.

Knock, knock.

Who's there?

Dishes.

Dishes who?

Dishes the last time I'll knock on your door.

FAMILY MATTERS

Knock, knock.

Who's there?

Nana.

Nana who?

Nana your business.

Knock, knock.

Who's there?

Honey.

Honey who?

Honey, I'm home.

Knock, knock.

Who's there?

Dishes.

Dishes who?

Dishes your mother. Open up.

Knock, knock.

Who's there?

Closure.

Closure who?

Closure mouth while you're eating, please.

Knock, knock.

Who's there?

Well not your parents

because they don't knock.

Knock, knock.

Who's there?

I'm T.

I'm T who?

Oh, you're only two? Is your mom home?

Knock, knock.

Who's there?

Cook.

Cook who?

Hey, I'm not crazy.

Knock, knock.

Who's there?

Cousin.

Cousin who?

Cousin my house, we open the door for family.

FUNNY PLACES

Knock, knock.

Who's there?

Hawaii.

Hawaii who?

Hawaii you? I'm fine.

Knock, knock.

Who's there?

Yukon.

Yukon who?

Yukon say that again.

Knock, knock.

Who's there?

Sweden.

Sweden who?

Sweden the coffee and open the door.

Knock, knock.

Who's there?

Amarillo.

Amarillo who?

Amarillo nice guy.

Knock, knock.

Who's there?

Irish.

Irish who?

Irish you would open the door.

Knock, knock.

Who's there?

Amish.

Amish who?

Really? You don't look like a shoe.

Knock, knock.

Who's there?

Safari.

Safari who?

Safari so good.

Knock, knock.

Who's there?

Adair.

Adair who?

Adair you to answer and find out.

Knock, knock.

Who's there?

Abyssinia.

Abyssinia who?

Abyssinia around lately.

Knock, knock.

Who's there?

Africa.

Africa who?

African love you.

Knock, knock.

Who's there?

Iran.

Iran who?

Iran all the way here; I'm tired.

Knock, knock.

Who's there?

Europe.

Europe who?

No I'm not.

Knock, knock.

Who's there?

Armegeddon.

Armegeddon who?

*Armegeddon a little bored.
Can you hurry up?*

CRYPTIC MUCH?

Knock, knock.

Who's there?

You know.

You know who?

Exactly.

Knock, knock.

Who's there?

Adore.

Adore who?

Adore stands between us. Open up.

Knock, knock.

Who's there?

Me.

Me who?

You don't know who you are?

Knock, knock.

Who's there?

Police.

Police who?

Police let us in; it's cold out here.

Knock, knock.

Who's there?

See.

See who?

See you if you'll let me in.

Will you remember me in a month?

Yes.

Will you remember me in a week?

Yes.

Will you remember me in a day?

Yes.

Knock, knock.

Who's there?

See. You forgot me already.

Knock, knock.

Who's there?

Spell.

Spell who?

W-H-O.

Knock, knock.

Who's there?

Tank.

Tank who?

You're welcome.

Knock, knock.

Who's there?

Ya.

Ya who?

Actually, I prefer Google.

Knock, knock.

Who's there?

Cargo.

Cargo who?

Nope. Cargo beep.

Knock, knock.

Who's there?

Thumping.

Thumping who?

Thumping green and slimy is climbing up your back.

Knock, knock.

Who's there?

Boo.

Boo who?

Well, you don't have to cry about it.

Knock, knock.

Who's there?

Little old lady.

Little old lady who?

Wow. I didn't know you could yodel.

Knock, knock.

Who's there?

You.

You who?

You who! Let me in.

Knock, knock.

Who's there?

Stopwatch.

Stopwatch who?

Stopwatch you're doing and open the door.

Knock, knock.

Who's there?

I O.

I O who?

Me. When are you paying me back?

Knock, knock.

Who's there?

Control freak.

Control freak wh–

Okay, now you can say, "Control freak, who?"

Knock, knock.

Who's there?

A broken pencil.

A broken pencil who?

Never mind. It's pointless.

Knock, knock.

Who's there?

Says.

Says who?

Says me.

Knock, knock.

Who's there?

CD.

CD who?

CD person on your doorstep?
That's me.

Knock, knock.

Who's there?

No one.

No one who?

...

IT'S NATURAL

Knock, knock.

Who's there?

Heart.

Heart who?

Heart to hear you. Can you speak up?

Knock, knock.

Who's there?

Water.

Water who?

Water these plants, or they're going to die.

Knock, knock.

Who's there?

Leaf.

Leaf who?

Leaf me alone.

Knock, knock.

Who's there?

Snow.

Snow who?

Snow use. I forgot my name again.

Knock, knock.

Who's there?

Wire.

Wire who?

Wire you asking? I just told you.

Knock, knock.

Who's there?

Cotton.

Cotton who?

Cotton a trap; can you help me out?

Knock, knock.

Who's there?

Ash.

Ash who?

Bless you. I did not mean to make you sneeze.

Knock, knock.

Who's there?

Wooden shoe.

Wooden shoe who?

Wooden shoe like to know?

Knock, knock.

Who's there?

Mustache.

Mustache who?

Mustache you a question, but I'll shave it for later.

Knock, knock.

Who's there?

Radio.

Radio who?

Radio not; here I come.

Knock, knock.

Who's there?

Comb.

Comb who?

Comb on down and I'll tell you.

Knock, knock.

Who's there?

Icy.

Icy who?

Icy you looking at me.

Knock, knock.

Who's there?

Hike.

Hike who?

I didn't know you liked Japanese poetry.

Knock, knock.

Who's there?

Tree.

Tree who?

Treemendous to see you again.

BEST. RIDDLES. EVER.

JOKES for KIDS

CHANTELLE GRACE

NATURE

1) I go up
   when rain comes down.
   What am I?

2) I am the ocean.
   Where can you find me
   without water?

3) In the dark I am found
   without being fetched.
   In the light I am lost
   without being stolen.
   What am I?

4) I am a shirt.
   If you drop me
   in the red sea,
   what do I become?

5) The boy, girl, and their dog
   weren't under the umbrella.
   Why didn't they get wet?

6) I have lots of eyes
   but cannot see.
   What am I?

7) I am the letter of the alphabet
that holds the most water.
What letter am I?

8) I go around and around
the woods,
but I never go
into the woods.
What am I?

9) I come out at night
without being called
and disappear during the day.
What am I?

10) I am the kind of tree
you can hold in your hand.
What am I?

*7) The letter C.   8) The bark on a tree.   9) The moon.
10) A palm tree.*

11) I am in the center of gravity.
   What am I?

12) A cloud is my mother,
    the wind is my father,
    my son is a puddle.
    A rainbow is my bed,
    and people often dislike me
    even though I am necessary.
    What am I?

13) When you take away more,
    I become bigger.
    What am I?

14) I have no feet, hands, or wings,
    but I fly to the sky.
    What am I?

15) I can be used to feed people,
    build houses, contain messages,
    and fertilize the ground.
    What am I?

16) If you feed me, I live,
    but if you water me, I die.
    What am I?

17) I am blue, red,
    and many other colors.
    I have no end,
    and no gold to find.
    I don't live in water or on land.
    If you could catch me,
    I would taste rather bland.
    What am I?

18) I grow in the winter
    but die in the spring.
    I am made of water
    but can hang upside down.
    What am I?

19) Before Mt Everest
    was discovered,
    I was the
    highest mountain
    in the world.
    What mountain am I?

20) You can see me in water,
    but I never get wet.
    What am I?

THE BODY

1) I have two legs
   but cannot walk.
   What am I?

2) I am a question
   you can never say yes to.
   What question am I?

3) When things go wrong,
   you can always count on me.
   What am I?

4) You can hear me,
   but you can't see or touch me
   even though you control me.
   What am I?

5) You can catch me,
   but you can't throw me.
   What am I?

6) I have teeth,
   but I cannot bite.
   What am I?

7) I am sitting in a dark house
   with no lights on,
   but I am reading.
   How is this possible?

8) I am as light as a feather,
   but even the world's strongest man
   can't hold me for more
   than a few minutes.
   What am I?

9) I have a thumb and four fingers
   but cannot pick anything up.
   What am I?

10) I am the best cure
    for dandruff.
    What am I?

7) I am reading Braille. 8) His breath. 9) A glove. 10) Baldness.

200

11) What do you call a man
who does not have
all his fingers on one hand?

12) I am the last thing you take off
before you get in bed.
What am I?

13) I have a bottom
at the top of me.
What am I?

14) I am moving left to right
and right to left
right now.
What am I?

11) Normal. (Most people have all their fingers on both hands.)
12) Your feet (off the floor). 13) Legs. 14) Your eyes.

201

15) I have legs but don't walk,
    a strong back but don't work,
    and two good arms
    but can't reach anything.
    What am I?

16) I have no legs,
    but I can run.
    What am I?

17) I weaken people
    for hours each day.
    I show you strange visions
    while you are away.
    I take you by night,
    by day bring you back.
    None suffer to have me
    but do from lack.
    What am I?

18) I have a tongue that can't speak,
    eyes that can't see,
    and a soul that can't be saved.
    What am I?

19) I run but never walk
    have a mouth but never talk.
    What am I?

20) A man walked all day long
    but only moved two feet.
    How is this possible?

AROUND THE HOUSE

1) I go up and down
   but never move.
   What am I?

2) I get wetter
   the more I dry.
   What am I?

3) I buried my flashlight.
   Why?

4) If a red house
   is made of red bricks,
   and a yellow house
   is made of yellow bricks,
   what is a greenhouse made of?

5) I'm tall when I'm young
   and short when I'm old.
   What am I?

6) I am full of holes
   but hold a lot of water.
   What am I?

7) I have legs
   but don't walk.
   What am I?

4) Glass. 5) A candle. 6) A sponge. 7) A table.

8) In a one-story pink house,
   there was a pink person,
   a pink cat, a pink fish,
   a pink computer, a pink chair,
   and a pink table.
   What color were the stairs?

9) I run along your property
   and all around the backyard,
   but I never move.
   What am I?

10) Imagine you're in a room
    that is filling with water.
    There are no windows or doors.
    How do you get out?

8) There weren't any stairs. It was a one-story house. 9) A fence.
10) Stop imagining.

206

11) If Mr. Red lives in the red house,
Mr. Green lives in the green house,
and Mr. Black lives in the black house,
who lives in the white house?

12) I have keys but no doors.
I have space but no rooms.
I allow you to enter
but you can't leave.
What am I?

13) I let you see
right through a wall.
What am I?

14) I have a neck, but no head.
What am I?

15) If you walked into a room
with a lantern, a candle,
and a fireplace,
what would you light first?

16) I have one eye
but can't see.
What am I?

17) I need an answer,
but I don't ask a question.
What am I?

18) I have 88 keys
but cannot open a single door.
What am I?

19) I can go up the chimney
    when I'm down,
    but I can't go down the chimney
    when I'm up.
    What am I?

20) I am a door,
    but sometimes I'm not.
    When would that be?

21) I am an empty pocket,
    but I still have something in me.
    What is it?

22) I am black, white
    and read all over.
    What am I?

19) An umbrella. 20) When I am ajar. 21) A hole. 22) A newspaper.

209

23) I leave home
and turn left three times,
only to return home
facing two men wearing masks.
Who are those men?

24) I make two people from one.
What am I?

25) I have no breath,
but I can die.
What am I?

26) Four rubber ducks
were floating in the bathtub.
Two floated away and two drowned.
How many ducks are still alive?

23) The catcher and the umpire. 24) A mirror. 25) A battery.
26) Zero. Rubber ducks aren't alive and they can't drown.

27) I have one head,
    one foot, and four legs.
    What am I?

28) I am a can that never
    needs a can opener.
    What am I?

29) I go up and down the stairs
    without moving.
    What am I?

30) I come in many different
    colors and shapes.
    I rise when I'm full
    but fall when I'm not.
    What am I?

31) I hang or stand by a wall,
run fast with hands
but have no feet at all.
What am I?

32) I always come into
the house through a keyhole.
What am I?

33) I come in different colors;
sometimes I am hot,
sometimes I am sweet.
I can't answer you because my bell
doesn't ring.
What am I?

34) I have feet on the inside
but not on the outside.
What am I?

IN THE KITCHEN

1) You have me for dinner
   but you never eat me.
   What am I?

2) I have to be broken
   before you can use me.
   What am I?

3) I am invisible.
   What do I drink at snack time?

1) Silverware. 2) An egg. 3) Evaporated milk.

4) I am a room
   with no doors.
   What kind of room am I?

5) I have many layers.
   If you get too close to me,
   I'll make you cry.
   What am I?

6) I am a cup,
   but I don't hold water.
   What kind of cup am I?

7) I am a type of cheese
   that is made backwards.
   What cheese am I?

8) I am two things
   you can never eat for breakfast.
   What am I?

9) I am put on a table and cut,
   but I am never eaten.
   What am I?

10) The sun bakes me.
    A hand breaks me.
    A foot treads on me.
    A mouth tastes me.
    What am I?

11) A car key opens a car;
    a house key opens a house.
    What opens a banana?

8) Lunch and dinner. 9) A deck of cards. 10) Grapes. 11) A monkey.

215

12) Tuesday, Sam and Peter
went out for pizza.
After eating, they paid the bill.
Sam and Peter did not pay the bill.
Who did?

13) You throw away the outside
and cook the inside.
You eat the outside
and throw away the inside.
What did you eat?

14) You cannot see me
nor can I be touched.
You cannot feel me,
but I can cook your lunch.
What am I?

ON THE JOB

1) I start with P, end with E,
   and have a million letters.
   What am I?

2) I start to work
   only after I have been fired.
   What am I?

3) I go up
   but never come down.
   What am I?

4) This is the only place
   success comes before work.
   Where?

5) I fell off a 20-foot ladder
   but I wasn't hurt.
   Why?

6) I am the time you know
   you have to go to the dentist.
   What time am I?

3) Your age. 4) In the dictionary. 5) I fell off the bottom step.
6) 2:30 (tooth-hurty).

7) What is the difference
between a jeweler and a jailer?

8) Today the sailors
couldn't play cards.
Why?

9) A lawyer, a plumber, and a hat maker
were walking down the street.
Who had the biggest hat?

10) If it takes six men one hour
to dig six holes,
how long does it take
one man to dig half a hole?

7) A jeweler sells watches. A jailer watches cells. 8) The captain was
standing on the deck. 9) The one with the biggest head.
10) There is no such thing as half a hole.

11) What did the outlaw get
when he stole the calendar?

12) I am taken from a mine
and shut up in a wooden case,
from which I am never released,
but I am used by almost everybody.
What am I?

13) A building has four floors.
The higher the floor,
the more people live there.
Which floor does the elevator
go to most often?

14) I shave over 25 times a day
but still have a beard.
What am I?

15) I work when I play
and I play when I work.
What am I?

16) If four people can repair
four bicycles in four hours,
how many bicycles can
eight people repair in eight hours?

14) A barber. 15) A musician. 16) Sixteen.

TRANSPORTATION

1) I am the only time
   you go at red
   and stop at green.
   What time am I?

2) A truck driver is going opposite
   traffic on a one-way street.
   A police officer sees him
   but doesn't stop him.
   Why?

3) I go up and down
   but never move.
   What am I?

4) I am an electric train
   heading south,
   which way is my steam blowing?

5) You walk across a bridge
   and see a boat full of people;
   yet there isn't a single person
   on board.
   How is this possible?

6) I go through towns and over hills,
   but I never move.
   What am I?

3) The temperature. 4) An electric train doesn't create steam.
5) All the people on the boat are married. 6) A road.

223

7) A cowboy rides into town on Friday,
   stays for three days,
   and leaves on Friday.
   How did he do it?

8) A man was driving his truck.
   His lights were not on.
   The moon was not out.
   Up ahead, a woman was
   crossing the street.
   How did he see her?

9) I am thrown out when you
   want to use me
   but taken in when you
   don't want to use me.
   What am I?

7) His horse's name was Friday. 8) It was daytime. 9) An anchor.

224

10) I am a ship with two mates
and no captain.
What ship am I?

11) I am so simple
that I can only point,
but I guide people
all over the world.
What am I?

12) I went out for a walk,
and it started to rain.
I didn't bring an umbrella or a hat.
My clothes got soaked,
but not a hair on my head was wet.
How is this possible?

AROUND THE WORLD

1) What nationality are you
   on the way to the bathroom?

2) What nationality are you
   while you are in the bathroom?

3) What nationality are you
   when you leave the bathroom?

4) How is Europe
   like a frying pan?

5) I have streets but no pavement.
   I have cities but no buildings.
   I have forests but no trees.
   I have rivers but no water.
   What am I?

SPORTS

1) I am a race that is never run.
   What kind of race am I?

2) I threw a ball as hard as I could.
   It didn't bounce off anything,
   but it came right back to me.
   How did this happen?

3) What did the baseball glove
   say to the ball?

4) You can you serve me
   but never eat me.
   What am I?

5) I am running in a race.
   I just passed the person
   in second place.
   What place am I in?

6) I am the fastest runner of all time.
   Who am I?

3) Catch you later. 4) A volleyball. 5) Second place.
6) Adam. (He was first in the human race.)

7) I am a boomerang
   that doesn't come back.
   What am I?

8) I love to move around,
   but usually not on the ground.
   I am strung out when way up high.
   I like to sail, but I need to stay dry.
   I need air, but not to breathe.
   A helpful hand is all I need.
   What am I?

7) A stick. 8) A kite.

ANIMALS

1) How far can a bear run into the woods?

2) How can a leopard change its spots?

3) I am black, white,
   and blue.
   What am I?

4) I am orange and green
   and sound like a parrot?
   What am I?

5) I give milk
   and I have a horn,
   but I'm not a cow.
   What am I?

6) I am a key
   that can't open any door.
   What am I?

7) I am a dog catcher.
   How do I get paid?

8) How many animals
   did Moses take on the ark?

9) I am a dog.
   What do I have
   that no other animal has?

10) A dog was on a 10-foot rope
    but it got to a bone
    that was 12 feet away.
    How did the dog get the bone?

7) By the pound. 8) Moses didn't take anything on the ark. Noah did. 9) Puppies. 10) The rope wasn't attached to anything.

233

11) I am a person,
    but sometimes I'm like a snake.
    When would that be?

12) I travel very slowly
    when gliding along the ground.
    Maybe my shell weighs me down.
    What am I?

13) I have two heads,
    four eyes, six legs,
    and a tail.
    What am I?

14) I am what chimpanzees
    use to fix a leaky faucet.
    What am I?

14) A monkey wrench.

11) When I am rattled. 12) A snail. 13) A cowboy riding his horse.

234

15) I can jump and I can climb.
    With my many legs,
    I swing from tree to tree.
    I can build a house
    much bigger than me.
    What am I?

16) I am the type of music
    that rabbits like.
    What am I?

17) I have four legs
    but no tail.
    You often only hear me at night.
    What am I?

18) I am the month of the year
when monkeys like to play
basketball.
What month am I?

19) There is a rooster on a roof.
If it lays an egg,
which way would the egg roll?

20) I peel like an onion
but still remain whole.
What am I?

21) I am always in armor,
but I've never been at war.
I have no sword, no bow, and no spear.
What am I?

18) Ape-ril. 19) Roosters don't lay eggs. 20) A lizard. 21) A turtle.

236

22) A farmer has seventeen sheep.
All but nine of them die.
How many sheep
does he have left?

23) I am a strange creature,
hovering in the air,
moving from here to there
with a brilliant flare.
Some say I sing,
but others say I have no voice.
What am I?

24) If three peacocks
lay five eggs in eight days,
how many peacocks
will lay 45 eggs
in 72 days?

22) Nine.   23) A hummingbird.   24) Peacocks don't lay eggs. Peahens do.

237

25) Emily loves cats and she
   keeps some as pets.
   All but two of them
    are completely black.
   All but two of them
    are completely white.
   All but two of them
    are completely ginger.
   How many cats does Emily have?

26) I am green
    but not a leaf.
    I copy others,
    but I'm not a monkey.
    What am I?

BACK TO SCHOOL

1) You see me once in June,
   twice in November,
   but not at all in May.
   What am I?

2) I am a word that
   becomes shorter
   when you add two letters.
   What word am I?

3) I am spelled wrong
   in every dictionary.
   What word am I?

4) A word I know,
   six letters it contains.
   Remove one letter
   and 12 remains.
   What word is it?

5) I contain 26 letters
   but only three syllables.
   What am I?

6) I am the month of the year
   that has 28 days.
   What month am I?

7) I am a band
   that never plays music.
   What am I?

8) There are four days of the week
   that start with the letter T.
   What are they?

9) I am the only place where
   Friday comes before Thursday.
   Where am I?

10) I begin and end
    with an E,
    but I only have one letter.
    What am I?

7) A rubber band. 8) Tuesday, Thursday, today, and tomorrow.
9) In the dictionary. 10) Envelope.

241

11) I can make one disappear.
How?

12) Why is the letter T
like an island?

13) I am an instrument
you can hear but never see.
What am I?

14) When I am white,
I am dirty,
and when I am black,
I am clean.
What am I?

11) I add a G and it's gone. 12) Because it's in the middle of water.
13) Your voice. 14) A blackboard.

242

15) Which is heavier:
a ton of bricks
or a ton of feathers?

16) How many letters are there
in the English alphabet?

17) I am a number.
Take away a letter
and I become even.
What number am I?

18) If two's company,
and three's a crowd,
what are four and five?

15) Neither, they both weigh the same.
16) 3 in "the," 7 in "English," and 8 in "alphabet." 17) Seven.
18) Nine.

243

19) Draw a line.
Without touching it,
how do you make it
a longer line?

20) Using only addition,
I add eight eights
and get the number 1,000.
How?

21) What do the numbers
one and eight have in common?

22) I have a large money box.
Roughly how many coins
can I place in my empty money box?

19) Draw a short line next to it, and now it's the longer line.
20) 888 + 88 + 8 + 8 + 8 = 1000. 21) They read the same right side up
and upside down. 22) Just one. After that, it will no longer be empty.

244

23) If you multiply me
by any other number,
the answer will always
remain the same.
What number am I?

24) I am a three-digit number.
My second digit is
four times bigger than
the third digit.
My first digit is three less than
my second digit.
What number am I?

25) How many seconds
are there in a year?

23) Zero. 24) 141. 25) Twelve. January 2nd, February 2nd...

245

26) A school orchestra with six musicians can play Beethoven's Fifth symphony in seven minutes and 23 seconds. How long would it take to play if they doubled the number of musicians?

26) The same amount of time. The length of the piece of music doesn't change.

246

IN THE FAMILY

1) Emma's parents have
   three daughters:
   Snap, Crackle and...?

2) Mary has four daughters.
   Each of her daughters
   has a brother.
   How many children
   does Mary have?

1) Emma. 2) Five. Each daughter has the same brother.

247

3) Two fathers and two sons
   go on a fishing trip.
   They each catch a fish
   and bring it home.
   Why do they only bring
   three fish home?

4) Two children are born
   in the same hospital,
   in the same hour, day, and year,
   have the same mother and father,
   but are not twins.
   How is this possible?

5) A mother had five boys:
   Moses, Tucker, Webster,
   Thomas, and...?
   Was the fifth boy's name
   Frank, Evan, or Alex?

3) *The men are a grandfather, father, and a son.* 4) *They are two of a set of triplets.* 5) *Frank. The first two letters of each boy's name begin with the first two letters of the days of the week.*

6) A girl is 13 years old.
   Her father is 40 years old.
   How many years ago was
   the dad four times as old
   as the daughter?

7) A family of five people drove in a car
   for 300 miles at an average speed
   of 50 miles per hour.
   For the whole journey nobody noticed
   that the car had a flat tire.
   Why didn't anyone notice?

8) Tom owns an antique grandfather clock
   made in the year 1877.
   How long is it designed to go
   without winding?

6) Four. When the girl was nine, her father was 36. 7) The spare tire was flat. 8) It's not designed to go without winding at all.

249

9) A girl was 10
    on her last birthday,
and will be 12
    on her next birthday.
How is this possible?

WORD POWER

1) I am so fragile
   that saying my name
   breaks me.
   What am I?

2) I am easy to get into
   but hard to get out of.
   What am I?

1) Silence. 2) Trouble.

3) I can be broken
   even if you never pick me up
   or touch me.
   What am I?

4) I am always in front of you,
   but I can't be seen.
   What am I?

5) I come once in a minute,
   twice in a moment,
   but never in a thousand years.
   What am I?

6) The more you take of me,
   the more you leave behind.
   What am I?

3) A promise. 4) Your future. 5) The letter M. 6) Footprints.

7) I am a word that looks the same
   backwards and upside down.
   What word am I?

8) If I have it, I don't share it.
   If I share it, I don't have it.
   What is it?

9) I am in seasons, seconds,
   centuries, and minutes,
   but not in decades, years, or days.
   What am I?

10) Forward I am heavy,
    but backward I am not.
    What am I?

11) I am always later
   and never present now.
   What am I?

12) The more of me there is,
    the less you see.
    What am I?

13) The rich men want me.
    The wise men know me.
    The kind men show me.
    What am I?

14) I have to be given
    before I can be kept.
    What am I?

15) I can bring a smile to your face,
a tear to your eye,
or even a thought to your mind,
but I can't be seen.
What am I?

16) I am greater than God,
more evil than the devil,
the poor have me,
the rich need me,
and if you eat me, you'll die.
What am I?

17) I am yours to own,
but others use me more.
What am I?

18) Everyone needs me,
asks for me,
and gives me away,
but almost nobody takes me.
What am I?

19) I am greater than gold
but cannot be bought.
I can never be sold,
but you can earn me if sought.
Though I can be broken,
I can still be fixed.
I'm not started by birth,
nor by death will I end.
What am I?

20) Can you rearrange the letters of
NEW DOOR to make one word?

21) I am a word of five letters.
   People eat me.
   If you remove my first letter,
   I become a form of energy.
   Remove the first two,
   and I'm needed to live.
   Scramble the last three,
   and you can drink me.
   What am I?

IT'S A MYSTERY

1) I am as small as an ant
   and as big as a whale;
   I can soar through the air
   like a bird with a tail.
   I can be seen by day
   and not by night;
   I can be seen
   with a big flash of light.
   I follow whoever
   controls me by the sun,
   but I fade away
   when darkness comes.
   What am I?

2) The Smith family is a
very wealthy family
that lives in a big, circular home.
One morning, Mr. Smith saw
a strawberry jam stain
on his new carpet.
Everyone had jam on their
toast that morning.
By reading the following excuses,
figure out who spilled the jam.
Mom: I was in the shower.
Billy: I was outside
playing basketball.
Maid: I was dusting the
floorboard corners.
Chef: I was making lunch.
Who is lying?

2) The maid. A circular house has no corners.

259

3) A boy was rushed to
   the hospital emergency room.
   The ER doctor saw the boy
   and said, "I cannot operate
   on this boy. He is my son."
   But the doctor was not
   the boy's father.
   How could that be?

4) In marble walls
   as white as milk,
    lined with skin
   as soft as silk,
    in a fountain
   crystal clear,
    a golden treasure
   does appear.
    There are no doors
   to this stronghold,
    yet thieves break in
   and steal the gold.
    What is it?

3) The doctor was the boy's mother. 4) An egg.

5) A man lives on the 40th floor
   of an apartment building.
   When it is raining
   and he needs to go out,
   he takes the elevator down
   and the elevator back up.
   If it's not raining,
   he can take the elevator down,
   but he has to use the stairs
   to get back to his apartment
   unless someone else
   is in the elevator.
   Why?

6) The Wilsons' puppy was
   stolen on Sunday.
   The police know who took it
   by these clues.
   Can you figure it out?
   John was cooking.
   Alexis was getting the mail.
   Avery was planting in the garden.
   Kelly was doing laundry.

6) Alexis is guilty. There is no mail delivery on Sundays.

5) The man is very short. If it's raining, he has an umbrella so he can
reach the button for the 40th floor. If someone is in the elevator, he
can ask them to push the button for him.

7) Two men play five
complete games of checkers.
Each man wins the same
number of games.
There are no ties.
How is this possible?

8) A man was going to town
with a fox, a goose,
and a sack of corn.
He came to a river which he had
to cross with a tiny boat.
He could only take one thing
across at a time.
He couldn't leave the fox
alone with the goose,
or the goose alone with the corn.
How did he get them all safely
across the river and into town?

7) The two men were not playing against each other.

8) The man took the goose over first and came back alone. Then he
took the fox across and brought the goose back. Then he took the
corn. He came back by himself and took the goose.

9) Some chemicals were stolen
from a chemist's lab one night.
The only evidence was a piece
of paper that had the names
of chemicals written on it.
The substances were nickel,
carbon, oxygen, lanthanum,
and sulfur. The chemist only
had three people come by his
lab on the day of the theft:
fellow scientist Claire,
his nephew Nicolas,
and his friend Marc.
The chemist knew who the thief
was right away.
How?

9) It was Nicolas. If you combine the abbreviations of the chemicals on
the paper, you get the name: Ni-C-O-La-S.

10) A Japanese ship was leaving the port.
The captain went to oil some parts
of the ship and took his ring off,
so it wouldn't get ruined.
He left it on his bedside table.
When he got back,
the ring was missing.
He thought of three crew members
who could be guilty. He went and
asked them what they were doing
when he was gone.
The cook said he was in the kitchen
getting dinner ready.
The engineer said he was in
the engine room.
The seaman said he was up
on the mast fixing the flag
because someone had put it on
upside down.
The captain knew right away
who the thief was.
How?

10) It was the seaman. The Japanese flag is white with a red circle in the
middle. It can't be hung upside down.

264

11) On the morning before
Christmas in NY,
a mother went shopping.
When she came home,
the food in the house was gone.
The youngest son said
he was watching TV.
The middle son said
he was exercising.
The oldest son said
he was mowing the lawn.
The dad said
he was reading a newspaper.
The mom knows who ate the food.
Do you?

11) The oldest son. The lawn doesn't need to be mowed in the winter in NY.

265

12) A man is trapped in a room.
The room has two possible exits:
two doors.
Through the first door there
is a room constructed from
magnifying glass.
The blazing hot sun instantly fries
anything or anyone that enters.
Through the second door
there is a fire-breathing dragon.
How does the man escape?

13) A woman was sitting in her hotel room
when there was a knock at the door.
She opened the door to see a man
whom she had never seen before.
He said, "Oh I'm sorry.
I thought this was my room."
He then left.
The woman went back
into her room and called security.
What made the woman
so suspicious of the man?

13) You don't knock on your own hotel door, so the man was probably lying.

12) He waits until nighttime and then goes through the first door.

266

SIGN LANGUAGE

1) What does this say?
   /R/e/a/d/i/n/g/

2) What does this say?
   STRAWBERRYcake

3) What does this say?
   sister

1) Reading between the lines. 2) Strawberry Shortcake.
3) Little sister.

267

4) What does this say?

L
A
Y
I
N
G
JOB

5) What does this say?

I RIGHT I

6) What does this say?

TOKEEPUCH

7) What does this say?

ESGG SGEG GEGS GSGE

4) Laying down on the job. 5) Right between the eyes.
6) Keep in touch. 7) Scrambled eggs.

268

8) What does this say?
   TOIMWN

9) What does this say?
   YYURYYUBICURYY4ME

10) What does this say?
    STOOD
    MISS

11) What does this say?
    POT OOOOOOOO

8) I'm in town. 9) Too wise you are; too wise you be. I see you are too wise for me. 10) Misunderstood. 11) Potatoes.

269

12) What does this say?
   GIVE
   GIVE
   GIVE
   GIVE

13) What does this say?
   OR OR NOTHING

14) What does this say?
   ZERO
   Ph.D.
   Ed.D

15) What does this say?
   1 END 3 END 5 END 7 END 9 END

15) Odds and ends.

12) Forgive. 13) Double or nothing. 14) Two degrees below zero.

270

16) What does this say?

ISSUES ISSUES
ISSUES ISSUES
ISSUES ISSUES
ISSUES ISSUES
ISSUES ISSUES

17) What does this say?

ECNALG

18) What does this say?

T
O
W
N

LANGUAGE EQUATIONS

Figure out what these shortened phrases say.

1) 24 H in a D

2) 64 S on a C B

3) 12 M in a Y

4) 31 D in D

5) 1000 Y in a M

6) 23 P of C in the H B

3) 12 months in a year.   4) 31 days in December.   5) 1000 years in a millennium.   6) 23 pairs of chromosomes in the human body.

273

7) 1 L Y E F Y

8) 18 H on a G C

9) 4 S (S S A W)

10) 12 D of C

7) 1 leap year every four years. 8) 18 holes on a golf course. 9) 4 seasons (spring, summer, autumn, winter). 10) 12 days of Christmas.

274

11) 3 S y O

12) 66 B of the B

13) 60 S in a M

14) 90 D in a R A

11) 3 strikes you're out. 12) 66 books of the Bible. 13) 60 seconds in a minute. 14) 90 degrees in a right angle.

275

15) 10 Y in a D

16) 366 D in a L Y

17) 4 Q to the G

18) 60 M in an H

15) 10 years in a decade. 16) 366 days in a leap year. 17) 4 quarts to the gallon. 18) 60 minutes in an hour.

276

19) 9 I in a B G

20) 4 Q in a F G

21) S W and the S D

22) 360 D in a C

19) 9 innings in a baseball game. 20) 4 quarters in a football game. 21) Snow White and the seven dwarves. 22) 360 degrees in a circle.

277

23) 12 in a D

24) 7 W of the W

25) 88 K on a P

26) 12 I in a F

23) 12 in a dozen. 24) 7 wonders of the world. 25) 88 keys on a piano. 26) 12 inches in a foot.

27) 8 L on a S

28) 100 C in a M

29) 3 F in a Y

30) 10 Y in a D

27) 8 legs on a spider.   28) 100 centimeters in a meter.   29) 3 feet in a yard.   30) 10 yards in a down.

279

BEST. ROAD TRIP. JOKES. EVER.

JOKES for KIDS

CHANTELLE GRACE

ON THE ROAD AGAIN

What goes through towns, up hills, and down hills but never moves?

The road.

What is the highest road?

The highway.

What do you get when two giraffes collide?

A giraffic jam.

Why did the zebra cross the road?

Because it was a zebra crossing.

Why did the rhino get a ticket?

He ran through the stomp sign.

What did the stoplight say to the car?

"Don't look, I'm about to change."

Why did the elephant cross the road?

Because the chicken retired.

Why did Superman cross the road?

To get to the supermarket.

Why did the rhino cross the road?

To prove to the possum that it could be done.

How does a snowman get around?

He rides an icicle.

Why did the horse cross the road?

Because somebody shouted hay.

How do billboards talk?

Sign language.

The taxi driver was good at his job.

He kept driving his customers away.

AT SEA

What does a houseboat turn into when it grows up?

A township.

What's the worst vegetable to serve on a boat?

Leeks.

What floats in water and wears a uniform?

A buoy scout.

What do you call discounts at the boat store?

A two for one sail.

What do you call it when one hundred people stand on a dock?

Pier pressure.

What happened to the sailor when he did poorly on a test?

He got C-sick.

What did the sailor say when he was accused of speeding on his boat?

"I did knot."

What did the sailor use to buy his boat?

Sand dollars.

What is another name for a captain of a sailboat.

A sails manager.

Where do sick boats go?

The dock.

If a boat could fly, where would it go?

An airport.

What is in the middle of the ocean?

The letter E.

Where did Bugs Bunny anchor his boat?

   At the what's-up dock.

What kind of candy would help
someone who fell off a boat?

   A lifesaver.

What runs but never walks?

   Water.

Why don't oysters share their pearls?

   Because they're shellfish.

Why did the lobster go red?

   It saw the ocean's bottom.

What kind of rocks are never found in the ocean?

Dry ones.

Why is the ocean measured in knots instead of miles?

They need to keep the ocean tide.

Why did the teacher dive into the ocean?

To test the water.

What do you use to cut the ocean in half?

A sea-saw.

What turtle is the easiest to see?

A sea turtle.

What is the most famous fish in the ocean?

The starfish.

Where does a killer whale go to the dentist?

The Orcadontist.

What puts white lines on the ocean?

An ocean liner.

How much money does a pirate pay for corn?

A buccaneer.

What kind of hair do oceans have?

Wavy.

Have you heard of seasickness?

It comes in waves.

What lies at the bottom of the ocean and twitches?

A nervous wreck.

What do you get when you throw one million books into the ocean?

Title waves.

What do you get if you cross an elephant with a whale?

A submarine with a built-in snorkel.

BY AIR

Heard about the pilot who decided to cook while flying?

It was a recipe for disaster.

Why couldn't the librarian get on the plane?

Because it was overbooked.

What kind of chocolate do they sell at the airport?

Plane chocolate.

What happens when you wear a watch on a plane?

Time flies.

Why did the airplane get sent to its room?

It had a bad altitude.

Where do mountain climbers keep their planes?

Cliffhangers.

What has a nose and can fly, but cannot smell?

A plane.

Why did the student study on a plane?

To get higher grades.

What do you get when you cross a dog and an airplane?

A jet setter.

What's gray and moves at one hundred miles an hour?

A jet-propelled elephant.

What do you call an elephant that flies?

A jumbo jet.

What happened to the guy who sued over his missing luggage?

He lost his case.

A photon was traveling through airport security. The TSA agent asked if he had any luggage. The photon said...

"No, I'm traveling light."

IN TRAINING

How does a train eat?

It chew chews.

When is a rabbit as fast as a train?

When it's on the train.

What did the train conductor get for her birthday?

Platform shoes.

How do trains hear?

With engineers.

How do you find a missing train?

Follow the tracks.

What do you call a train that sneezes?

Achoo-choo train.

Why was the train late?

It kept getting side-tracked.

What is as big as a train, but weighs nothing?

Its shadow.

Why don't elephants like trains?

They can't leave their trunks in the baggage car.

Why was the train humming?

It didn't remember the words to the song.

HORSE AND CART

Why did the pony have to gargle?

Because it was a little horse.

When does a horse talk?

Whinney wants to.

What do you call a horse that lives next door?

A neigh-bor.

What's the best way to lead a horse to water?

With lots of apples and carrots.

What disease was the horse afraid of getting?

Hay fever.

How long should a horse's legs be?

Long enough to reach the ground.

Why did the man stand behind the horse?

He was hoping to get a kick out of it.

Which horse is the most mysterious?

Black Beauty. He's a dark horse.

What does it mean if you find a horseshoe?

Some poor horse is walking around in his socks.

What do you call a well-balanced horse?

Stable.

What do you give a sick horse?

Cough stirrup.

What's a horse's favorite sport?

Stable tennis.

What is the difference between a horse and a duck?

> One goes quick and the other goes quack.

What is the difference between a horse and the weather?

> One is reined up and the other rains down.

Why do cowboys ride horses?

> Because they're too heavy to carry.

Why did the horse eat with its mouth open?

> Because it had bad stable manners.

What do you call a horse that can't lose a race?

Sherbet.

What street do horses live on?

Mane St.

What did the mare tell her filly after dinner?

Clear the stable.

Where do horses go when they're sick?

The horsepital.

What kind of bread does a horse eat?

Thoroughbred.

CROSS COUNTRY

Which state is the happiest?

Merry-land.

What did Dela-ware?

A New Jersey.

Which state is the loudest?

Illi-noise.

What state is round on the outsides and high on the inside?

Ohio.

What did Tennessee?

The same as Arkansas.

Where do math teachers go on vacation?

Times Square.

Where do crayons go on vacation?

Color-ado.

Where do you go to dance in California?

San Frandisco.

What state produces cheese?

   Swiss-consin.

What is a horse's favorite state?

   Neighbraska.

Which state does the most laundry?

   Washington.

What has four eyes but can't see?

   Mississippi.

Where do eggs go on vacation?

   New Yolk City.

Which state is the smartest?

> *Alabama because it has four As and one B.*

What would you call the US if everyone lived in their cars?

> *An in-car-nation.*

Why is it so easy to get into Florida?

> *Because of all the keys.*

What state makes the country's pencils?

> *Pennsylvania.*

Where do horses get their hair done?

Maine.

Which state is famous for its small soft drinks?

Mini-soda.

Where do cows go on their summer vacation?

Moo York.

What is a lion's favorite state?

Maine.

Why did the cow go to California?

To see where moovies are filmed.

Where do pianists go for vacation?

Florida Keys

What rock group has four men who don't sing?

Mt. Rushmore.

AROUND THE WORLD

What travels around the world but stays in one corner?

A stamp.

What did the Pacific Ocean say to the Atlantic Ocean?

Nothing. It just waved.

Where is the biggest rope in the world?

Europe.

Where can you find the biggest pans in the world?

Japan.

Where do pirates go for vacation?

Arrrgentina.

Which country is the fastest?

Russia.

What country leaves the biggest mark?

Denmark.

What's the coldest country in the world?

Chile.

What country does Hungary eat?

Turkey.

Are you going to visit Egypt?

I sphinx so.

Do you want to eat your food here?

No, I want it Togo.

What do you call the little rivers that flow into the Nile?

Juveniles.

Is traveling to Costa Rica expensive?

It costa fortune.

Why is England the wettest country?

Because royalty has reigned there for years.

Where does pizza go on vacation?

The Leaning Tower of Pizza.

Where do sheep go for vacation?

The Baahamas.

Where do sharks go on vacation?

Finland.

Where do hamsters go on vacation?

Hamsterdam.

Where do bees go on vacation?

Stingapore.

Where does a bird like to travel?

The Canary Islands.

What is an ant's favorite vacation spot?

Frants.

What do you call a French man in sandals?

Phillipe Phloppe.

What do you take on a trip to the desert?

A thirst-aid kit.

What did the envelope say to the stamp?

"Stick with me and we'll go places."

What do you call a Spanish man who lost his car?

Carlos.

What do you call an elephant at the North Pole?

Cold.

Did you know French fries weren't actually cooked in France?

They were cooked in Greece.

Which country's capital has the fastest growing population?

Ireland. Every day it's Dublin.

What city cheats on tests?

Peking.

Visitors to Cuba are usually...

Havana good time.

I have a lengthy article on Japanese Sword Fighters...

I can Samurais it for you.

England doesn't have a kidney bank.

It has a Liverpool.

He said he was from South America.

I said, "I don't Bolivia."

Italian building inspectors in Pisa...

are lenient.

In a Scandinavian race, the last Lapp...

crossed the Finnish line.

Goats in France are musical.

They have French horns.

Things made in Australia...

are high koala-ty.

If you Russia round and Ukraine
your neck...

don't Crimea River.

I would like to go to Holland one day.

Wooden shoe?

When I go to West Africa...

I'm Ghana make sure Togo to Mali and
then I can say I've Benin Timbuktu.

There is some Confucion about...

the oldest religion in China.

Television sets in Great Britain...

have to cross the English Channel.

You don't know anything at all about ancient Egypt?

Tut, tut, tut.

The pharaohs of Egypt...

worked on the first pyramid scheme.

Which country has the most germs?

Germany.

Where were donuts first made?

In Greece.

Why did the Romanian stop reading?

To give her Bucharest.

If you send a letter to the Philippines...

you should put it in a Manila envelope.

People are happy when they vacation in Ireland.

They're usually walking on Eire.

People in Switzerland learn to ski...

with a lot of alp.

The US government has a lot of red tape.

In Scotland, they use Scotch tape.

MAP IT OUT

Why are maps like fish?

They both have scales.

What kind of map plays CDs?

A stereo map.

Why was the map gesturing wildly?

It was an animated map.

What do you get when you cross a farm animal with a map maker?

A cowtographer.

What does a great sportsman and map key have in common?

They're legends.

What do you call a man on top of a hill?

Cliff.

Did you hear the mountain joke?

No one can get over it.

Why are rivers rich?

They have two banks.

What do you find in the middle of nowhere?

The letter H.

What is a mountain's favorite type of candy?

Snow caps.

What did one volcano say to the other?

"I lava you."

Why are mountains the funniest place to travel?

They're hill areas.

TO THE MECHANIC

What has three letters and starts with gas?

A car.

What is a car's favorite meal?

Brake-fast.

Why should you check your car's tires for holes?

Because there might be a fork in the road.

What part of the car is the laziest?

The wheels because they're always tired.

When is a car not a car?

When it turns into the driveway.

What do you call a man with a car on his head?

Jack.

Why couldn't the car play soccer?

It only had one boot.

What was wrong with the wooden car?

It wooden go.

Why did the mechanic sleep under the car?

He wanted to wake up oily.

What has four wheels and flies?

A garbage truck.

Where do old Volkswagen cars go?

The old Volks home.

What happened when the frog's car broke down?

He started to jump it.

What made the dinosaur's car stop?

A flat Tireannosaurus.

My sister told me I couldn't make a car out of spaghetti.

You should have seen her face as I drove pasta.

I'm trying to make a car without wheels.

I've been working on it tirelessly.

I couldn't figure out how to buckle my seat belt.

Then it clicked.

WEATHER FORECAST

How does a hurricane see?

With its eye.

What happens before a candy storm?

It sprinkles.

When does it rain money?

When there is change in the weather.

What did one lightning bolt say to the other?

"You're shocking."

What type of cloud is lazy because it never gets up?

Fog.

What does the cloud wear under its pants?

Thunder-wear.

What's worse than raining cats and dogs?

Hailing taxis.

What bow can't be tied?

A rainbow.

What do clouds do when they're rich?

They make it rain.

What did the tornado say to the sports car?

"Want to go for a spin?"

Can bees fly in the rain?

Not without their yellow jackets.

What do you call it when it rains chickens and ducks?

Foul weather.

What did one blade of grass say to the other about the lack of rain?

I guess we'll just have to make dew.

I tried to catch the fog the other day.

I mist.

TROPICAL VACATION

Two waves had a race, who won?

They tide.

What did the beach say when the tide came in?

"Long time no sea."

What is brown, hairy, and wears sunglasses?

A coconut on vacation.

What kind of tree can you hold in your hand?

A palm tree.

What do you pay to spend a day on the beach?

Sand dollars.

What is the best kind of sandwich for the beach?

A peanut butter and jellyfish.

What's the best day to go to the beach?

Sun-day.

What did one tide pool say to the other?

"Show me your mussels."

Why do bananas use sunscreen at the beach?

Because they peel.

Why couldn't the two elephants go swimming together?

Because they only had one pair of trunks.

What does bread do on vacation?

It loaves around.

What's black and white and red all over?

A sun-burned zebra.

What does Cinderella wear when she goes to the beach?

Glass flippers.

What does the sun drink out of?

Sunglasses.

Why can't basketball players go to the beach?

They'd get called for travelling.

What kind of shoes does a person wear on a vacation?

Loafers

Why did the robot go on a beach vacation?

He needed to recharge his batteries.

What does Baloo the Bear pack for a trip to the beach?

Just the bear necessities.

What do frogs like to drink on a hot summer's day?

Croak-a-Cola!

How do rabbits get to their beach vacation?

By hare-plane!

CAMPOUT

How do you start a fire using two pieces of wood?

Make sure one is a matchstick.

Can a frog jump higher than a tent?

Of course. Tents can't jump.

What did one campfire say to the other?

"Do you want to go out tonight?"

Did you hear about the fire at the campsite?

It was intents.

What's another name for a sleeping bag?

A nap sack.

Why does Humpty Dumpty love camping in autumn?

Because he had a great fall.

Why are people who go camping on April 1st always tired?

Because they just finished a 31-day March.

What is a tree's favorite drink?

Root beer.

What did the doctor tell the camper when he went to the hospital?

You're two tents.

What did the alpaca say to his owner before camping?

"Alpaca tent."

If you have five tents in one hand and three in the other, what do you have?

Very big hands.

What color is the wind?

Blew.

What do you call a camper without a nose and a body?

Nobody nose.

Why do trees have so many friends?

Because they branch out.

Why are hiking shops so diverse?

Because they hire people from all walks of life.

I didn't like the romantic tree movie.

It was far too sappy.

How do you keep your sleeping bag
from getting stretched out?

Don't sleep too long in it.

If you're in the woods, how can you tell
if a tree is a dogwood?

By its bark.

What do bears call campers
in sleeping bags?

Soft tacos.

If you're on a hike and find a fork in the
road, what do you do?

Stop for lunch.

You can't run through a campsite.

> *You can only "ran" because it's past tents.*

I went to buy camping camouflage yesterday.

> *I couldn't find any.*

The seaside camping trip was so boring.

> *One day the tide went out and never came back.*

If you get cold while camping, sit in the corner of a tent.

> *It's usually 90 degrees.*

FISHING TRIP

What does a lion do on a canoe?

Use his roar.

Why did the melon jump into the lake?

Because he wanted to be a watermelon.

What did the beaver say to the tree?

"It's been nice gnawing you."

How do you avoid getting swallowed by a river while kayaking?

Stay away from its mouth.

What is a fisherman's favorite show?

The Reel Life.

How do you catch a fish without a fishing rod?

With bear hands.

Do fish go on vacation?

No, because they're always in school.

What do you call waiting five hours to catch a fish on a boat?

Quick.

Why do oars fall in love?

Because they're rowmantic.

WILDLIFE
SIGHTINGS

What's a frog's favorite car?

A beetle.

What is a sheep's favorite car?

A Lamborghini.

What kind of cars do snakes drive?

Anahondas.

What kind of cars do dogs hate?

Corvets.

What do you call it when dinosaurs crash their cars?

Tyrannosaurus wrecks.

Why are pigs bad drivers?

They hog the road.

Where do dogs park their cars?

The barking lot.

What is a cow's favorite holiday?

Moo Year's Eve.

Why did the spider cross the road?

To get to her website.

What do you call a flying primate?

A hot air baboon.

Why did the whales cross the ocean?

To get to the other tide.

What is gray, has four legs and a trunk?

A mouse on vacation.

What do you say to a frog who needs a ride?

"Hop in."

Where did the goldfish go on vacation?

Around the globe.

Why do elephants have trunks?

Because they would look funny with a suitcase.

What did the elephant say to her son when he was naughty in the car?

"Tusk tusk."

What do you call a bee that can't make up its mind?

A maybe.

PACK A BOOK

Traveling

by Anna Plane

Parachuting

by Hugo First

I Need Insurance

by Justin Case

Flying for Beginners

by Landon Safely

Where to Stay while Traveling

by Moe Tell

Vacation Budgeting

by Seymour Forles

How to Sail

by Boe Ting

A Perfect Day for Sailing

by Wynn Dee

Runaway Horse

by A. Tailov Woh

Daddy Are We There Yet?

by Miles Away

Stop Arguing

by Xavier Breath

Downpour

by Wayne Dwops

Life in Chicago

by Wendy City

Sea Birds

by Al Batross

Danger

by Luke Out

I'm Fine

by Howard Yu

Get Moving

by Sheik Aleg

I Must Fix the Car

by Otto Doit

Why Cars Stop

by M.T. Tank

It's Unfair

by Y. Me

Falling Trees

by Tim Burr

I Love Crowds

by Morris Merrier

Highway Travel

by Dusty Rhodes

Without Warning

by Oliver Sudden

You're Kidding

by Shirley U. Jest

I Say So

by Frank O. Pinion

Mountain Climbing

by Andover Hand

Equine Leg Cramps

by Charlie Horse

Exercise on Wheels

by Cy Kling

In the Arctic Ocean

by Isa Berg

Turtle Racing

by Eubie Quick

Almost Missed the Bus

by Justin Time

Where to Find Islands

by Archie Pelago

French Overpopulation

by Francis Crowded

The Excitement of Trees

by I. M. Board

Bundle of Laughs

by Vera Funny

WE'VE ARRIVED

Knock, knock?

Who's there?

Alaska.

Alaska who?

Alaska later, right now I'm busy.

Knock, knock.

Who's there?

Norway.

Norway who?

Norway am I telling you any more knock, knock jokes.

Knock, knock.

Who's there?

Oman.

Oman who?

Oman, these jokes are bad.

Knock, knock.

Who's there?

Kenya.

Kenya who?

Kenya think of a better joke?

Knock, knock.

Who's there?

Francis.

Francis who?

Francis a country in Europe.

Knock, knock.

Who's there?

Canoe.

Canoe who?

Canoe come over and play?

Knock, knock.

Who's there?

Avenue.

Avenue who?

Avenue heard this joke before?

Knock, knock.

Who's there?

Water.

Water who?

Water way to answer the door.

Knock, knock.

Who's there?

Havana.

Havana who?

Havana good time and wishing you were here.

Knock, knock.

Who's there?

Ida.

Ida who?

It's pronounced Idaho.

Knock, knock.

Who's there?

Juneau.

Juneau who?

Juneau the capital of Alaska?

Knock, knock.

Who's there?

Oslo.

Oslo who?

Oslo down. No need to hurry.

Knock, knock.

Who's there?

Venice.

Venice who?

Venice mom coming home?

Knock, knock.

Who's there?

Cargo.

Cargo who?

Cargo better if you fill it with gas first.

Knock, knock.

Who's there?

Iona.

Iona who?

Iona new car.

Knock, knock.

Who's there?

Isabel.

Isabel who?

Isabel necessary for riding a bike?

Knock, knock.

Who's there?

Ivan.

Ivan who?

Ivan working all day.

Knock, knock.

Who's there?

Levin.

Levin who?

Levin on a jet plane.

Knock, knock.

Who's there?

Philip.

Philip who?

Philip my gas tank, please. I've got a long way to go.

LICENSE PLATES

On a Tesla:

OIL LOL

On an Infiniti:

N BYOND

On a Ferrari:

ESCUZME

On a smart car:

OH I FIT

On a Saab:

WHASAAB

On a Delorean:

TIMELESS

On a VW Beetle:

EW A BUG

On a yellow car:

PIKACHU

On a Cube:

RUBIX

WRITE YOUR
FAVORITE JOKE HERE